Original title:
Purpose: The Last Piece of the Puzzle

Copyright © 2025 Creative Arts Management OÜ
All rights reserved.

Author: Olivia Sterling
ISBN HARDBACK: 978-1-80566-014-9
ISBN PAPERBACK: 978-1-80566-309-6

Where the Pieces Align

In a box, I found a sock,
It didn't fit, but it could rock.
A puzzle missing one last square,
Turns out, it's hiding everywhere!

I searched the floor, then under chairs,
A cat is purring, it just stares.
With every twist, each goofy grin,
Who knew that chaos could begin?

The Final Touch

A jigsaw on my kitchen floor,
With chips and crackers at the core.
I reached for wisdom through the snack,
But found a mystery—my brain's lack!

Each piece I tried, just didn't match,
A unicorn? A gourmet batch?
'Just one more piece,' I sighed and stared,
Then realized it was unprepared!

Discovering What Remains

I thought I'd found my missing chunk,
But it was just an old sock trunk.
The pieces strewn from here to there,
I laughed, then combed my wild hair.

With every turn, some snacks I see,
While hunting hard for destiny.
A rubber duck? A tiny shoe?
I guess this puzzle made me blue!

The Keyhole of Understanding

A key I found, but what's the lock?
Maybe it opens a giant clock?
The pieces twirl, they dance in line,
Yet every one is not quite fine.

Oh, the thrill of searching deep,
For things that hide—like dreams we keep.
My slippers' lost, but here I tread,
With laughter, joy, and bits of thread.

Mapping the Unseen

In the attic, maps unfold,
X marks the spot, or so I'm told.
With a compass, I spin in place,
But found only dust and a sad old vase.

My friends all laugh, they point and tease,
"You can't find shoe prints, just some bees!"
Yet, a treasure chest, under a bed,
Out pops a sock, 'Nah, not quite gold instead!'

The Lens of Clarity

Woke up one day with glasses on,
Saw the world fresh, like a brand-new dawn.
But all I found were dirty dishes,
And a stray cat making some odd wishes.

With lenses clear, I thought I'd see,
A bright future, just for me.
Instead I tripped over my own two feet,
And spilled my coffee, oh, what a treat!

In Search of the Unbroken

Looked for answers in the fridge at night,
Hoping for clarity, oh, what a sight!
Instead, I found snacks holding a wine line,
Cried, 'What's unbroken, I must define!'

Hunted for wisdom beneath the couch,
Found lost remotes and an old, furry grouch.
In the depths of chaos, there shone a light,
Turns out it was just my pizza slice, bright!

Breathing Life into Chaos

In the morning rush, I'd laugh and yell,
Finding my shoes, like a treasure spell.
One's in the kitchen, one's in the loo,
Guess it's just chaos trying to break through.

Gave up on order, let laughter in,
Danced with laundry in a battle to win.
Life's puzzle fits, but I see quite clear,
It's just too funny to take it severe!

Mosaics of Meaning

In a world of mismatched socks,
I search for what unlocks.
A jigsaw with a hint of flair,
My coffee cup, my favorite pair.

With puzzles flipped and colors bright,
I trip on thoughts in plain sight.
A shoe in hand, the dog's in charge,
This quest is weird, but strangely large.

The Final Heartbeat

A heartbeat bounces off the wall,
Like rubber ducks that seem to call.
Each thump a giggle, last and light,
I dance with shadows, oh what a sight!

Did I forget that missing tune?
The rhythms lost amidst the moon.
A final laugh, the grand reveal,
A punchline tossed, the best appeal.

Tuning into the Unfinished

An orchestra of chaos plays,
With out-of-tune and silly ways.
The conductor waves a fuzzy wand,
And narwhals prance across the pond.

Strumming strings of half-formed dreams,
I find the humor in the seams.
Where laughter meets the quirky sound,
The missing notes are still around.

Resounding Echoes of Truth

Echoes bounce like ping-pong balls,
Each truth dances, stumbles, falls.
I chase them down the winding hall,
As they giggle, daring me to call.

With whispers loud and chuckles tight,
The wisdom hides, a cheeky sprite.
In every corner, they take flight,
While I juggle my thoughts, what a sight!

The Missing Link of Existence

I searched for meaning in a sock,
A match to pair, a mystery lock.
My life's a puzzle, pieces fly,
Why do they vanish? Oh me, oh my!

The cat stole my thoughts, so much fun,
It's hard to think when on the run.
I traced my steps, found crumbs instead,
Leading to chaos, not wisdom's thread.

What's missing from this jumbled heap?
Is it a laugh or a chance to sleep?
In every gap, a giggle waits,
Perhaps the puzzle's tied with plates!

So here I am, quite a sight,
Searching for sense, a comedy light.
With every twist and every turn,
I find the laugh; let my heart yearn!

Threads of Destiny Unraveled

Tangled yarns, a crafty mess,
Life's like knitting in a stress.
I dropped a stitch while chasing dreams,
Now my sweater's full of seams!

Little hints in socks I've lost,
Direction's shifting, at what cost?
Is fate a thread, or just a joke?
Stitching laughs, or is it a poke?

In my closet, chaos reigns,
A dance of fabric, some faux chains.
Could laughter be the missing thread?
Or just my shirt now seen as red?

Let's untangle these colorful strands,
Find joy in knots, wherever it lands.
Oh, what a sight, my wardrobe's flair,
Destiny's threads are everywhere!

Quest for Meaning's Fragment

Once I thought I'd find it here,
A clue, a sign, or even a beer.
I quested hard, oh such a trip,
Ended up with a pizza slip!

Maps were drawn with crayon fun,
A treasure hunt for everyone.
But each step led me to mischief,
With pies to eat, my spirit's gift.

In gardens wild, I lost my mind,
Floral meanings, quite unkind.
Did I seek wisdom or a snack?
This search for truth went quite off-track!

Yet in the chase, a chuckle grew,
The fragment's not what I once knew.
It's not the end; it's laughs unplanned,
In every twist, life's silly brand!

The Final Shape of My Journey

Winding roads with twists and turns,
The end's a shape that rarely learns.
I sought a sign, a glowing star,
But tripped on air, oh how bizarre!

Each step I took, a playful dance,
In puddles laughed, my silly chance.
The road was long, the snacks divine,
With fries and jokes, my heart did shine.

At every corner, giggles found,
Shapes of laughter spinning 'round.
Who needs a map? Just join the fun,
In this odd journey, I have won!

The final shape is joy on feet,
A path of giggles, oh so sweet.
So let's embrace this wacky ride,
For every twist, I take with pride!

Threads of the Universe

In a world of mismatched socks,
I search for meaning through the flocks.
A puzzle piece that doesn't fit,
Like trying to bake with just a bit.

I tried to dance but lost my shoe,
Twisted my hair, oh, what a view!
The cat just laughed, my dog just snored,
They've got the secrets I'd adored.

A hotdog flew, who knew the sky?
The universe just winked an eye.
I think my brain just took a break,
And left me here to bake a cake.

But in this chaos, laughter blooms,
Like socks that find their way to rooms.
Each thread I tug brings joy anew,
Is it madness? Nah, just my view!

Shadows of the Incomplete

In the corner of my living room,
Lies an incomplete jigsaw's gloom.
One piece missing, where could it be?
The cat claims it's now part of she.

I chase my thoughts like paper planes,
Through sunny skies and rainy stains.
But figuring it out's a riddle,
Like trying to play a tune on a fiddle.

My refrigerator hums a tune,
While I scour the house, amiss in noon.
A shadow darts; I give a chase,
It's only my sock, a mischievous race.

But maybe pieces don't always align,
Like two end pieces sipping wine.
Incomplete? Oh, that's just grand!
I can dance; it's my one-woman band.

The Last Stanza of the Song

I strum my guitar, but it squeaks,
As I search for rhymes, it's all peaks.
The last stanza is playing hide and seek,
Like a squirrel on caffeine, oh so chic!

My lyrics dance like fireflies,
But often they just up and fly.
Singing high notes, losing my breath,
A melody that teeters on the edge of death.

I call my friends for some support,
They're busy with a cat debate on sport.
"Should I keep singing?" I skeptically ask,
"Just add some jazz, that's your real task!"

So I'm mixing beats, it's quite absurd,
Crafting a song with just one word.
Laughter breaks, that's where it's strong,
The final note bursts in a joyful throng!

Beyond the Last Step

I climbed up high to find some shoes,
They dangled there, like scandalous views.
One last step and oh, what a fate,
I tripped on my dreams and landed late.

The ladder creaked like a song of glee,
As I whispered, "Can't someone help me, please?"
But my sandwich was too busy to care,
It's hard to listen when you're in a dare!

I stretched my arms for one last try,
Grabbed at nothing, turned to the sky.
The lawn gnomes chuckled, quite the sight,
Are they wise or just full of spite?

But maybe the trip was meant to show,
That laughs are brighter when life's in tow.
So I'll keep stepping, fall or rise,
Finding joy beyond the surprise!

Whispers of a Silent Mission

In shadows where the laughter hides,
A secret dance that fate abides.
Chasing socks and missing keys,
We stumble through with jolly ease.

The cat's the mastermind, you see,
Plotting schemes while sipping tea.
With toys that squeak and beds that flop,
Our mission? Nap or make a mop!

Unfolding the Canvas of Intent

With crayons drawn across the floor,
A masterpiece behind the door.
Each stroke a giggle, brush a treat,
A canvas made for tiny feet.

The dog paints tales of fishy dreams,
While squirrels plot their nutty schemes.
Intentions lost like crumbs in sand,
Artistry led by a furry hand.

A Tapestry of Dreams Completed

Weaving thoughts with threads so bright,
A tapestry spun in morning light.
Each knot a laugh, each twist a grin,
Stitching together the chaos within.

The hamster rolls in circles tight,
Chasing dreams beneath the night.
With yarn scattered all about,
Our masterpiece? A cozy rout!

Echoes of the Unsung Truth

In the attic where dust bunnies roam,
Echoes of giggles find their home.
A treasure hunt for socks and shoes,
The truth is hidden in silly clues.

The plants conspire in their own way,
With whispers of mischief day by day.
Their leaves might flutter, watch them prance,
Unraveling secrets with every glance.

Silent Revelations Beneath the Surface

In the depths of a cereal bowl,
A goldfish plots its escape.
It dreams of a candy land,
But splashes upon an old grape.

With bubbles like secret whispers,
It tickles the cat's twitchy nose.
Finding joy in the oddest places,
Where pudding and ketchup both pose.

Pondering why socks disappear,
In the spin cycle's wild dance.
Perhaps they're off to a sock party,
Somewhere in a vibrant expanse.

Each lost foot is a mystery,
A riddle without a guile.
Maybe they're working in pairs,
On a grand sock fashion style.

The Last Stroke of the Creator's Brush

With a wobbly hand and some paint,
A masterpiece starts to emerge.
An elephant strides on a canvas,
While a frog yodels, ready to surge.

Canvases smell of fresh chaos,
As colors collide without care.
The brush thinks it's Picasso,
But only smudges are there!

The artist drops a slice of pie,
And it lands in a puddle of hue.
'What a tasty abstraction!' they cry,
While squirrels applaud with a view.

Each stroke is a tickle, a laugh,
A dance on the verge of delight.
Let mistakes become pages of art,
As the studio bursts into light!

Pieces of the Grand Design

Fit the puzzle pieces just right,
Said the cat as it chewed on the edge.
With a meow and a flick of its tail,
It declared, 'I'm the puzzle's true pledge!'

Grandma's knitting yarns in the way,
Threads mingle and tangle like fate.
'Tis a blanket of laughter,' she chuckles,
While knitting up stories so great.

The dog thinks it's all a game,
Chasing bits as they fly through the sky.
'What's the end?' it barks in despair,
'Will we find that last piece by and by?'

It's a quest, an odd trivia night,
With mismatched pieces galore.
Life's jigsaw just keeps coming,
Who knew chaos could be such a score?

In Search of the Unseen Compass

I set out on a quest for the truth,
With a rubber duck as my guide.
It quacked in directions so funny,
And swayed like it was full of pride.

Where the wildflowers twist and twirl,
And the butterflies join in the dance.
A compass so wobbly and bright,
Who knew adventure could take such a chance?

The stars giggled above with glee,
As I duck-waddled through the wood.
'Just a little mischief!' they winked,
'Hope you find what's under the hood!'

A treasure of hugs and bright laughter,
Maps drawn in crayon on the way.
It turns out the fun was the journey,
And the quack that brightened the day.

Pieces of the Infinite

In a box, I found a jigsaw bright,
Each piece danced like it was out of sight.
I tried to place them, one by one,
But all I got was a puzzle of fun!

Corners missing, sides all askew,
I laughed so hard, my face turned blue.
A cat jumped in, thinking it's a game,
Now all the pieces look quite the same!

Finding pieces, a comical chase,
Through laughter, I found a missing place.
With goofy shapes, I've lost my way,
Yet joy's the answer, come what may!

Gathering Fragments of Light

Collecting shards of a sunlight beam,
I slipped and fell—oh what a scream!
A prism of giggles, shining bright,
   With every piece, I took flight!

A feather here, a sparkle there,
I gathered laughter, light as air.
Tripping on clouds, what a delight!
I'll chase the rainbows, day and night!

Fragments twirling, in a crazy mix,
With every stumble, I find my fix.
In the chaos, I've made it right,
Turns out the chase is pure sunlight!

Transcending the Maze

In a maze of cheese, I tried to roam,
With every turn, I missed my home.
Rats laughed while I spun around,
Yet in that laughter, joy was found!

Maps are tricky when cheese is king,
I called for help, heard faint voices sing.
They squeaked advice, I took their lead,
Found my way with a joyful speed!

A maze of giggles, a cheesy place,
Each twist and turn, a smile on my face.
In getting lost, I learned a ton,
Who knew the maze could be so fun?

The Unlocking of the Heart

I found a lock, rusted and old,
Thought it held treasure, riches untold.
With a grin, I jiggled the key,
Turns out it opened my soup recipe!

Like unlocking joy in a silly way,
My heart laughed loud, come what may.
Old memories danced, twinkling bright,
Suddenly soup seemed out of sight!

So here I stand with a pot on the stove,
Mixing my laughter, my secret grove.
In every giggle, the key finds its part,
Turns out the best is the unlock of the heart!

The Dawn of Clarity

In the morning light, I found my sock,
A sock that once fit, now a ticking clock.
With every step, it gave a cheer,
Who knew lost things could be so dear?

From crumbs of toast to missing spoons,
They all unite, like silly cartoons.
One day I'll find that puzzle piece,
A match made in breakfast time's sweet peace.

Yet laughter rises like warm, fresh bread,
How can I ponder when joy's widespread?
So I dance about, both spry and sprightly,
For clarity waits, though it teases politely.

The day rolls on with giggles and grins,
Mixing the chaos with playful spins.
Life's a jigsaw in a funny frame,
And oh, how we dance, just the same!

The Touch of the Spirit

A ghost in the fridge, what a strange sight,
Whispering secrets in the pale moonlight.
It jostles the jars, causing great frights,
Yet it brings out the laugh on our late-night bites.

A flick of the toaster, a dance in the air,
While bread takes flight, without a care.
It's not just the snack; it's the spirit we share,
That makes kitchen chaos a game so rare.

The cat joins the fun, with mischief entwined,
Chasing the shadows it hopes to blind.
In every mishap, a giggly cheer,
Bringing us closer as we shed a tear.

From spirits to snacks, life's a banquet grand,
With every odd puzzle, we make our stand.
Embrace the absurd, let laughter flow free,
For the touch of the spirit is all we need!

Even the Gaps Belong

In every masterpiece, a gap we find,
Like a face without brunch; how unrefined!
The missing parts tell their own tale,
Like socks in the dryer; a balmy gale.

Between pieces of laughter and playful jests,
Even the gaps can be lovely guests.
They poke and they prod, like a friend so bold,
In the space between, stories unfold.

Searching for wisdom, I step on a block,
My foot finds a tune, it starts to mock.
With wiggles and wiggles, I dance round the room,
Embracing the gaps, banishing gloom.

So raise a toast to the missing and bare,
For even the gaps have something to share.
In life's grand mosaic, each piece is a song,
And that's why, my friend, even gaps belong!

The Celestial Compass

I took out my compass, it led me astray,
Pointing to pizza, what a strange play!
North, South, East, and a piece of pie,
Who knew the stars would make me fly high?

The moonbeams giggle and twinkling stars,
Guide me through life, past all of the bars.
With every wrong turn, I find a new treat,
The universe chuckles, what could be sweet!

In the quest for direction, I found my own path,
With laughter as fuel, I can't help but laugh.
Each twist and each twirl, a whimsical dance,
Thanks to the compass that leads me to chance.

So follow the stars, let the laughter ring,
For even the silly can lead to a king.
In the compass of fun, we all have a stake,
And the maps that we make, keep us awake!

The Heartbeat of My Aspiration

In a land where socks go missing,
I search for dreams and ambition,
With a cereal box as my throne,
I ponder life's grand composition.

My goldfish gives me thumbs up,
As I try to fix the mess,
But he just swims in circles,
In a watery state of stress.

I'll trade my Wi-Fi for a chance,
To dance with fame, or at least with cheese,
But mice on stage take all the glance,
While I'm lost in laughter's breeze.

So hand me that pizza slice,
The one with quirky toppings galore,
Let's figure this out in a trice,
And maybe find what we adore.

Fragments of a Greater Whole

In a jigsaw made of chocolate,
I seek to find a missing piece,
The cat just licked my project late,
Now I'm left snacking, oh what a tease!

The clock is ticking, can't you see?
But tick-tock goes a faulty gear,
Perhaps a dance will set me free,
Or at least distract from impending fear.

I once thought about a kite,
But it flew into a burger stand,
Now it just swings left and right,
In search of fries, as I had planned.

Each crumb reveals a deeper thought,
About life's wibbly constraints,
As I realize I'm distraught,
But hey—at least I have these paints.

Shadows Dancing in the Spotlight

Underneath the disco ball,
My shadow twirls with utmost grace,
Yet the floor gives me a sudden call,
And I find myself lost in space.

The audience throws popcorn at me,
Thinking it's part of the grand show,
But I'm just here to spill my tea,
In a salsa with a side of woe.

I swear this dance has meaning,
Like a cryptic puzzle of sorts,
But my feet keep intervening,
And the music abruptly cavorts.

Yet in the chaos, joy is born,
In the laughter, I lose my fear,
No perfect moves, just my scorn,
But each slip brings the crowd near.

The Alignment of Stars and Ambitions

When the stars align for a split second,
I stumble upon a cosmic joke,
A chicken crossed the road, and then
A comet zoomed past like smoke.

I raised my glass to the finesse,
Of dreams that aim for bizarre heights,
But gravity had its own stress,
And I ended up with pizza bites.

Celestial bodies give me hope,
With their twinkles and oddball spins,
Yet here I am with a slippery rope,
Tied to my favorite pair of twins.

So let's pitch a tent in the sky,
And camp 'neath weird astrological claims,
For even if we aim too high,
We might just end up winning games.

The Final Brushstroke

A canvas full of colors bright,
Swirls of chaos, what a sight!
But where's the corner with that lore?
Oh wait, I spilled some paint galore!

Frantic strokes, oh what a race,
I paint a bunny, or is it space?
The masterpiece is far from done,
Oh look, a cat! No, just a bun!

One last touch, shall it be neat?
A dash of orange, dark with heat.
But what if I miss that last flare?
And turn my canvas into despair!

In the end, it's just for fun,
A splash of joy, we've just begun.
With laughter echoing in each hue,
Is that confusion, or genius too?

Embracing the Unfinished Symphony

Notes are flying, like a bird,
Wait, where's the beat? That's just absurd!
A trumpet blares, but wait—uh oh!
That sounds more like a cow's sad 'Moo!'

Are we in tune? Or is it chaos?
A polka beat, or just plain gloss?
The flutes are lost in cosmic dust,
Or maybe they're just out on a bust!

The conductor's waving like a pro,
Yet all I feel is a funky flow.
Is this a symphony or a game?
Each squeak and honk—are we to blame?

Finally, we join with glee,
Playing wild, just like the sea.
Unfinished tunes, a hoot and cheer,
The music's silliness, oh dear!

The Essence of Completion

In a world of missing socks and shoes,
Where did I put that bottle of blues?
I search for order in this mess,
But find more chaos, I confess!

I start a puzzle, piece by piece,
Fifty pieces, not a lease!
Where's that edge? Oh, what's the plan?
I think I saw it, or was it spam?

Count the seconds, wasting time,
As I consider this a crime.
The final piece is a magic game,
Can't find it still, oh what a shame!

Yet through the stress, I find some cheer,
The wobbly table held so dear.
In the chaos, there's pure delight,
Each missing piece a wacky sight!

In Search of Lost Meaning

Where's the purpose, like a sock?
A treasure hunt, please take stock.
Should I check the fridge or under the bed?
Or is it hiding inside my head?

I ponder deeply, drink my tea,
What's the meaning? Is it just me?
A game of hide-and-seek with fate,
The clock says run, but I just wait!

I trip on thoughts, stumble on jest,
Is it pizza rolls or the big quest?
As I wander through this messy maze,
Found a lost burger? What a phase!

In the confusion, smiles arise,
Life's a riddle in silly disguise.
Stop the quest, embrace the strange,
For laughter's the meaning of every change!

The Heart of the Matter

In the center lies a heart,
Beating rhythm, a quirky art.
With socks misplaced and shoes askew,
We laugh at what we thought we knew.

Puzzle pieces tossed about,
Trying hard to figure out.
A spatula in a puzzle box,
What's the use of all those socks?

Chasing dreams in silly hats,
Slipping on some runaway cats.
The rainbow juice spills on the floor,
Who knew a wrench would open doors?

With laughter loud and joy in tow,
Finding meaning in the flow.
Each mishap leads us to the grin,
As we embrace the world we're in.

Threads of Intention

In a fabric store, I made a thread,
Snagged it up while toeing the lead.
With colors popping, bright like confetti,
I pondered how it all fits, just steady.

Twisting yarn with quite a flair,
Knots and tangles everywhere!
The only thing I held so tight,
Was a cat that took off in fright.

Stitching dreams with buttons and lace,
Finding humor in this wild race.
Each knot I made a giggling jest,
Who knew the fabric of life's a test?

And when it all unwinds so fast,
I'll smile and giggle, have a blast!
For every thread has its own spin,
In this crazy game, let's dive in!

Secrets of the Unseen Path

Wandering down a twisty lane,
Where ducks wear hats and cows complain.
I found a sign that said 'this way',
But it led to pancakes — hooray!

In the woods, the trees do gossip,
Whispering secrets, never stop.
Raccoons with shades sing across the brook,
The pathway's map is quite the book.

Mysteries wrapped in a bubble gum,
Guiding us like a grilled cheese drum.
I stumbled on a field of dreams,
Where nothing's ever quite what it seems.

Roads uncharted hold the jest,
Where silly paths can be the best.
With every step, there's joy to find,
Laughter echoes, a sugar rush kind!

Mapping the Uncharted

With a compass spinning round and round,
I plotted dots on the lost and found.
The map was scribbled in crayon bright,
Leading laughs into the night.

X marked the spot for chocolate treats,
Hidden under imaginary seats.
The treasure trove was full of glee,
But discovered by a mischievous bee!

Adventure calls with a noisy clang,
Landing me right in a giant tang.
Yet every twist and turn I take,
Brings joy along with each silly break.

So let's explore this crazy ride,
With wobbly maps and jokes as our guide.
For in the quest for the unknown path,
Laughter's found, and that's the math!

Harmony in Discord

In a room filled with noise, they all chime,
A kazoo and a trumpet, oh, what a crime!
Cat on the piano, dog plays a drum,
Together they bicker, but they still hum.

Yet every wrong note feels oddly right,
Their chaos spins out in broad daylight.
To find a sweet sound, they sort through the din,
While the cat just dreams of where to begin.

With laughter so loud, the neighbors all stare,
Perhaps there's a method with madness to share.
So amidst the discord, they grin and they dance,
Searching for rhythm, perhaps in a trance.

In the heart of this ruckus lied something profound,
A quirky connection that quietly bound.
In the wackiest ways, joy found its sway,
Who knew deranged harmony could save the day!

The Unveiling of Truth

Behind the curtain, a mystery brews,
An insightful old sage or a man in big shoes?
He pulls out a coin, flips it with flair,
Turns out it's just gum stuck deep in his hair!

As the crowd leans in, whispers abound,
What is the truth that he's finally found?
With a wink and a nod, he's all set to share,
A knock-knock joke; truth fills up the air!

"Knock, knock," he starts; they all shift in their seats,
"Who's there?" they reply, as if itching for sweets.
"Alpaca," he quips, but before he can finish,
The audience giggles, and the moment can't diminish.

In laughter, he knows what his wisdom can bring,
For truth's just a riddle wrapped up in a zing.
And though he will stumble, he stands tall and proud,
In his silly shenanigans, he's loved by the crowd!

Echoes of Fulfillment

In the kitchen, the pots all sing loud,
While the recipe's lost, much to the chef's crowd!
Flour is flying like a snowstorm in May,
'Tis a cake of confusion, or so they all say.

As batter spills over, they laugh 'til they cry,
"The oven's confused; it thinks it can fly!"
But out comes a treat, not quite as they planned,
A three-layer mishap—the chef waves his hand.

Sayers of wisdom pile into a queue,
"Just add more icing; it's perfect, who knew?"
With each melting layer, the echoes resound,
In laughter and sweetness, fulfillment is found.

They feast on their cake, it's almost a dream,
With sprinkles of joy, they all break at the seam.
In the chaos they created, they dance and they play,
And in every sweet bite, their troubles decay!

The Angle that Illuminates

A corner of the room claims it knows best,
With pictures hung crooked, it's quite the jest.
A table lamp's flickers make shadows that twist,
The angles confuse, like a plot that is missed.

But behind the odd angles of furniture stacked,
Lies a treasure trove of laughter untracked.
As friends gather 'round, their stories collide,
Who knew rearranging could make hearts confide?

With the cat on the shelf and a dog in the chair,
Each joke that is told fills the air with good cheer.
The angle that seems askew offers a gift,
In laughter, in chaos, their spirits uplift.

So in the odd corners where shadows take flight,
Friendship finds joy in the curves of the night.
And who would have thought with a quirky design,
That angles of laughter can truly align?

Pieces of My Soul

In quirky corners, I find my heart,
Missing bits make it a work of art.
A jigsaw puzzle, all jumbled up,
With pieces sticking out like a puppy's pup.

Each whimsy chunk, a tale to tell,
Like socks that hide in laundry hell.
I laugh as I shuffle, a hilarious dance,
Will I ever get my pieces in a chance?

A left foot here, a right hand there,
It's total chaos, but I don't care.
With a twist of fate and a giggle or two,
I'll make my soul fit, how about you?

So here's to life's crazy patchwork scene,
Each missing piece, a chance to glean.
With a knowing grin, let's play this game,
Finding joy in the hunt, never the same.

The Final Puzzle Shape

The last piece lurks, what a silly sight,
A triangle in a square's long fight.
It laughs at the logic, a quirky tease,
Cuz we all know shapes exist to please.

I look for edges, and then for flat,
But this sneaky piece says 'I'm not that!'
With colors so bold, it's a party, you see,
Mixing and matching, how wild can we be?

The frame is done, but wait—what's this?
A smiley face bursting from the abyss.
It wiggles and jigs as if to say,
"Who needs to fit in? Let's dance today!"

So gather your shapes, let's not be glum,
In this crazy world, be a little numb.
Take that last piece, make your own way,
For laughter and joy—hip, hip, hooray!

Unraveling the Great Design

With threads like spaghetti, twisted and tight,
I tug on the fabric with all my might.
What's woven within, a tapestry bright,
Is it a masterpiece or just a plight?

Knots of mystery, like socks in the wash,
The colors collide, like an artist's splosh.
Each whimsical twist tells a tale, oh dear,
Of why I lost my left shoe last year.

In a web so grand, I can't find my jam,
A chicken, a squirrel, oh where is my ham?
The yarn keeps unwinding, a comical chase,
Like wanting a hug in the wrong kind of place.

So let's stitch these stories with laughter and cheer,
Embrace all the threads that brought us here.
We're weaving a journey, so let's not forget,
That life's a big quilt, with no room for regret.

The Thread of Destiny

A thread so thin, it's barely there,
Pulling me onward, yet full of flair.
It dances and wiggles, a mischievous line,
Leading me places, both yours and mine.

With a tug and a twist, it shapes my day,
Making plans go astray in a funny way.
"What's next?" I ponder, with a chuckle or two,
The thread just winks, 'I'm not done with you.'

Through ups and downs, it dangles and sways,
Telling me stories in wobbly ways.
It takes me on journeys that often surprise,
Like wearing mismatched socks, oh my, what a prize!

So let's grab this thread, give it a spin,
With laughter and joy, let the fun begin.
For life's all a tangle, but here's the decree—
Embrace every twist, and just let it be.

Beneath the Veil of What Could Be

In a world of socks, mismatched and bright,
I ponder my fate by the fridge late at night.
Yet I find myself chasing that elusive cheese,
Could a slice bring me joy? Oh, if only I please!

Waking up daily, my coffee runs cold,
Heart set on dreams that are daring and bold.
Yet the cat on my lap steals the seat that I crave,
While I plot my escape like a whimsical knave.

Plans made on napkins, they flutter and fly,
Each one like a bird, with a thought or a sigh.
What if I dance? What if I sing?
Perhaps I'll find solace in the chaos they bring!

So here's to the jigsaw of upside-down fun,
As I giggle with glee, it's my game to be won.
The puzzle is wild, with each piece I explore,
Finding joy in the journey and laughing for more!

Harmonizing Dreams into Reality

In the realm of the absurd, where ducks like to chase,
I try to catch dreams, but they're all over the place.
Each whimsy diverges, a wacky parade,
Yet I hold onto laughter, it's my best escapade.

I sing to my plants, though they seem unimpressed,
Harmonizing life with each wiggle and jest.
A pot of gold waiting, yet still full of grime,
Maybe I'm just practicing a whimsical rhyme.

Chasing my goals with a goofy old stunt,
Like juggling spaghetti while leapfrogging a runt.
Reality ticks by, but I'm dancing around,
Each twirl is a dream, unconfined and unbound!

With a laugh and a wiggle, I zip through the day,
Finding joy in the chaos, come what may.
Because life's little puzzles are best when they're fun,
Who needs a map? I'll just follow the sun!

The Final Note of Life's Melody

In the concert of chaos, a cat gives a meow,
Conducting my laughter and solemnly now.
A tuba on fire, a kazoo in my hand,
With absurdity soaring, I'm taking my stand.

The last note approaches, oh what will it be?
Will I nail the crescendo or fall into glee?
With each silly stumble, each blunder, each giggle,
I strum to the rhythm of life's awkward wiggle.

As the curtain draws close and the stand-ins all cheer,
I tip my hat proudly, refusing to fear.
Who knew that a jester could teach me so much?
That living is play and laughter's the touch!

So I'll laugh in the face of a giggling fate,
For every misstep just opens the gate.
To a world full of wonders, both wacky and grand,
I'll sing my last note with a confetti-filled hand!

Constellations of a Purposeful Heart

Underneath a sky where the pizza stars shine,
I ponder my dreams and sip fizzy wine.
Each slice holds a secret, a wish set afloat,
If only my heart had an on-a-whim boat!

The cosmos are weird, with their wobbling dance,
Making shapes in the sky that beg for a chance.
I'd twirl with the pandas and tango with ducks,
While weaving through shooting stars and unicorn trucks!

In the constellation of quirky delight,
I find my own rhythm and dance through the night.
Balancing giggles as I float through the dark,
Each star a reminder of my unique spark.

So raise up a toast, with a grin ear to ear,
For every zany wonder that brings us good cheer.
With a heart full of whimsy, come take my hand,
Let's chart a wild course to dreamland, oh so grand!

The Symphony of Meaningful Connections

In the orchestra of life, we play our roles,
With mismatched socks and half-baked goals.
A triangle tango, a square-dance to boot,
Who knew being lost could feel so acute?

The tuba toots loudly, the flute plays it sweet,
While the trombone just slides like it's got cold feet.
We laugh as we fumble, yet find the right beat,
Connecting each note, our vibe is elite.

Through banter and giggles, we craft our refrain,
With a dash of chaos and a sprinkle of pain.
We're all in this symphony, a wild charade,
Laughing at life as we serenade.

At the end of the concert, we raise up a cheer,
The band of misfits, where smiles reappear.
In this symphony's madness, we found our own way,
Strumming through life like it's our cabaret!

A Journey to Uncharted Realms

Off we go, on a quest so absurd,
With a map made of jelly and spaghetti blurred.
We'll ride on our llamas through untraveled lands,
With GPS guided by questionable hands.

We'll stumble on treasures, or socks at the least,
In valleys of laughter, where troubles are ceased.
Finding a burrito beneath a great tree,
In uncharted realms, it's just you and me.

With quests full of giggles and snacks on our backs,
We conquer the wild and dodge all the quacks.
No dragons to slay, just a dance-off perhaps,
In the kingdom of nonsense, we'll take all the naps.

At the end of the route, we'll cheer and proclaim,
"We did it all wrong but we'll still take the fame!"
For journeys like this are rich without gold,
In uncharted realms, it's the stories we hold.

The Puzzle Box of My Soul

My heart's like a puzzle, all jumbled and lost,
With pieces from childhood and dreams that embossed.
A corner from Christmas, a side from my nerd,
And what's this weird piece? Oh, that's just my word.

I flip and I rotate, it's twisty and bright,
A wild combination, oh what a sight!
Did I mention the cat that once stole a part?
Now he sleeps on the bits of my too-busy heart.

Each piece tells a story, some sunny, some blue,
I oft mix 'em up, can't discern the true hue.
Like a jigsaw of life, I fit like a glove,
In this chaotic place, I'm still searching for love.

And though I may sigh when they don't seem to fit,
I laugh at the mess—there's joy in the split!
So I'll cherish each fragment, both silly and wise,
In the puzzle box of my soul, that's where joy lies!

Where Questions Find Their Answers

Why do we wonder about socks in the wash?
Or where did the goldfish go? Did he squish and squash?
In the realm of the wacky, where giggles are free,
I ponder the meaning while sipping my tea.

What's the secret of life? Is it cake or the maze?
Or is it just laughter that brightens our days?
I question the cosmos, imagine the quest,
Sometimes I just stare at the ceiling and rest.

With queries galore and a heart full of dreams,
I scribble my thoughts in fanciful themes.
The answers are silly, like unicorns prance,
In a world full of logic, I still choose to dance.

In this whimsical quest where the strange feels quite right,

I'll gather the riddles, under stars shining bright.
For here in the madness, my doubts take their flight,
In a land of confusion, I'd say it's all light!

Born from the Gaps

In the chase for meaning, what a spree,
I lost my socks, and now it's just me.
Chasing the cat, where's my shoe?
Turns out, life's answers are in tuna stew.

With jigsaw pieces, I made a kite,
Flapping away, oh what a sight!
Stuck in the tree, it seems so clear,
The more I search, the more I cheer.

Bitten by dogs, and laughed at by goats,
It's a tough life, but I've got my quotes.
Life's a puzzle, that's no lie,
A riddle wrapped in a pizza pie.

An Invitation to the Unknown

Packing my bags for the great unknown,
What did I forget? Oh, my phone!
Grabbed some snacks, and my best hat,
I'm off to find what's more than that.

Maps are confusing, but that's okay,
I'll follow the ducks and find my way.
Through fields of candy, and rivers of soda,
I'll run till I find my own smoked feta.

But do I have to wear shoes? Oh geez!
These toes were meant for the sun and breeze.
With sparkly socks and a wig on my head,
I'll take on the world, fueled by cheese spread.

The Bridge to Clarity

Building a bridge with spaghetti and glue,
Hoping it holds while I take a view.
Will it be sturdy? I don't really know,
Maybe it's better as a plate for my dough.

Crossing my fingers, it starts to lean,
What a fine line between sweet and obscene!
But making mistakes can be quite the thrill,
Especially when you tumble down the hill.

With a splash in the puddle, I rise up with glee,
Life's all about noodles and slippy debris.
So let's bridge the gaps with laughter and fun,
And embrace our quirks while on the run!

Illuminating Shadows

Caught in a shadow that dance with the night,
I grabbed my flashlight, oh what a sight!
Turns out it was just my old cat named Lou,
Who prances and prattles as if he's a shoe.

With bright ideas both silly and vivid,
I chased my old thoughts, so weirdly hid.
Searching for answers in joke books and dreams,
This silly adventure is bursting at the seams!

Through giggles and whispers, I've come to find,
Life's just a circus, oh so unlined.
So grab your own shadow, give 'em a spin,
And boldly step out, let the laughter begin!

Chasing the Faded Dreams

I once chased clouds on a sunny day,
With ice cream hands, I slipped away.
The dreams were gone, but I still ran,
In flip-flops, laughing, a quirky plan.

I found a sock in a tree so high,
Thought it was part of my grand sky.
But all I caught was a silly grin,
While birds above were laughing in.

So here I am, with no grand scheme,
Just humming tunes of my daydreams.
Who knew a chase could be this fun?
In a world where the socks out-run!

And every step a comic fluke,
With daffodils and a rubber duke.
Just chasing faded dreams of yore,
While life hands me laughter at the door.

The Last Thread of Connection

In a room full of wires, I found a string,
Tangled connections of everything.
I pulled a bit, heard a funny beep,
Maybe that's where my lost socks creep.

I chatted with a lamp that flickered bright,
Claimed it knew how to dance all night.
With each twist and turn, I lost my way,
Finding my path in a light ballet.

A toaster chimed in, sharing its dreams,
A world of butter, toast, and creams.
We laughed and joked, a cozy crew,
Awkward moments, but funny too.

So if you're lost in the messy fray,
Seek the simple, in a smile's way.
The last thread connects through silly schemes,
In a world that sparkles with funny dreams.

Gathering the Stars

I tried to gather stars in a jar,
But they winked and giggled from afar.
I tossed a net, but caught a breeze,
Dancing under the cosmic tease.

The moon just sighed, 'What a good try!'
As I flopped about while aiming high.
With a laugh and a hop, I hit the ground,
In a puddle of stardust, I spun around.

So I painted skies with coffee spills,
And tripped over moonbeams, oh the thrills!
A star or two fell into my shoe,
I wore them proud, with a cosmic view.

In this playlist of laughter, I found my tune,
Among twinkling lights and a rambunctious moon.
Gathering stars is a silly art,
Especially when they play the heart.

Cracking the Code of Existence

I sat with a puzzle, pieces galore,
The picture formed as I snacked on more.
With every bite, a new thought danced,
Cracking the code, I was entranced.

A cat walked by, claimed the lost square,
Catching bits of laughter in the air.
From oranges to socks, life felt like play,
Finding joy in the jumbled display.

I turned it upside down, what a mess,
But it showed a face of happiness.
In riddles and giggles, we found our way,
In the chaos, there's magic each day.

So here's to the puzzles we try to unfold,
With quirky pieces and stories untold.
Cracking the code in a world so bright,
Finding fun in the tangled delight.

Fractals of Faith

In a world of quirky shapes,
We search for that missing bit,
A puzzle piece shaped like cake,
But it's really just a script.

The corner's always out of reach,
A joke we fail to get,
As the cat spins in a screech,
Chasing tails without a net.

With every twist and turn we make,
Lost in a tangle of delight,
Where's the missing slice of cake?
I think it's gone to take a flight!

Fractals twirl like whirlybirds,
Making sense of giggling craze,
Life's riddles hang like silly words,
But we dance through the puzzling maze.

The Dance of Completion

A jig of joy, a skip of fun,
We gather pieces, one by one,
To form a picture, bright and neat,
While mismatched socks discriminate our feet.

In a ballroom filled with blank stares,
We swing and twirl, forget our cares,
A two-step tango with empty space,
Who said a puzzle's a serious race?

One sock hops, while the other droops,
Can't find the edge, just silly loops,
We laugh as the clock spins sideways,
And celebrate our quirky ways!

The music fades, but we're not done,
We'll jive until the morning sun,
For every piece that's out of sight,
We dance with joy, and it feels just right.

The Whispering Core

Amidst the shadows, whispers play,
A puzzle's heart in disarray,
It nudges me with playful tease,
"Just fit me in, and you'll feel ease!"

Round and round, I spin about,
Searching for pieces, there's no doubt,
A missing bit that giggles loud,
Like a gremlin hiding in a crowd.

Spinning wheels of thought and care,
Making sense seems quite a dare,
But oh, that core, it knows the tune,
Is it a fish or a silver spoon?

With each odd turn, I trip and fall,
Yet laughter rises, a joyous call,
I'll chase that whisper, giggle and grin,
'Cause finding the core is where we begin!

Shattered Reflections

In mirrors cracked, the truth can hide,
A jigsaw face with no inside,
I search for me, with puzzled glare,
But all I find is just thin air.

A mirror ball spins party vibes,
Colorful shards make silly jibes,
"Hey, is that your nose or mine?"
Giggles echo, we toe the line.

Reflection's game of cloak and play,
What's real? What's a ghost today?
In shattered pieces, laughter sings,
Amongst the shards, joy truly springs.

So join the dance of broken glass,
Where every defect holds a sass,
In this madcap puzzle we call life,
We'll laugh and twirl, devoid of strife.

Chasing the Essence of Why

Why do chickens cross the street?
To find the answers, not just to eat.
A quest for meaning, or just a jest,
Everyone's searching for their own little quest.

In a world of questions, we spin around,
Searching for wisdom that can't be found.
With every turn, we laugh and trip,
Chasing our tails in a comical skip.

The ducks are quacking with stories to share,
While squirrels debate if they should have flair.
Each nut collected, a mission so grand,
Nature's own punchline, it's all unplanned.

So let's all ponder, with giggles and glee,
What's the reason for life? Oh, can't you see?
We're all just puppets in a grand ol' play,
Dancing in circles, come what may!

Reflections in the Labyrinth of Life

In the mirror maze, there's a twist of fate,
Which way to go? I'm never late!
Each reflection laughs, distorting my face,
In a world of echoes, I lose my place.

I ask the shadows for a little advice,
They joke and they giggle, oh, isn't it nice?
"Turn left, then right, and just take a chance,
Maybe you'll find your own funky dance!"

As I wander through corridors, I lose my stride,
Every corner I turn, I'm filled with pride.
A jesting journey with friends made of light,
We stumble and fumble, all through the night.

With every wrong turn, there's a chuckle or two,
Life's maze is silly; who knew it was true?
And though we're lost, we'll just ride it out,
Laughing together, that's what it's about!

The Hidden Key to Tomorrow

I searched for the key in my kitchen drawer,
Among pots and spoons, oh, what a chore!
Maybe it's hidden behind all that grunge,
Or perhaps, it's just like my morning grunge.

Peering through piles of yesterday's cake,
Who knew finding answers could make my head ache?
A sprinkle of wisdom rests under the bread,
But first, I'll need coffee – or so it is said.

The toaster speaks up, "It's all in the heat!"
"Find joy in the crunch, it's a scrumptious feat."
With each slice I toast, ideas start to flow,
Tomorrow's key lies in butter and dough.

So I'll bake some muffins, with laughter and cheer,
And giggle at life's mysteries as they appear.
For what more is there than finding the fun?
Turning crumbs into joy, one laugh at a pun!

Navigating the Maze of Wishes

In the land of wishes, I wander and roam,
Through fields of dreams, I make my home.
With a map upside down, it's quite a sight,
Each crossroad's a riddle, a silly delight.

One wish leads to another like a chain of cheese,
I chase after whims, but they're never at ease.
A squirrel whispers secrets—I've lost track of time,
He says, "Just enjoy it; this maze is sublime!"

With wishes like bubbles, they float in the air,
I reach out to catch them, but they vanish with flair.
Each giggle's a treasure, each stumble a gem,
In this twisty adventure, I'm not just a whim.

So let's conjure our longings and dance on our toes,
Navigating the maze, where the wild laughter flows.
In the silliness of wishes, who needs a plan?
Life is a puzzle, let's have some fun, if we can!